ALSO BY LAURENCE CARR

Fiction and Poetry:
Pancake Hollow Primer (novel)
Threnodies, poems in remembrance (poems)
The Wytheport Tales (poems and prose poems)

Dramatic Works:
Kennedy at Colonus: The Journey of Robert F. Kennedy
Vaudeville
The Voyage of Mary C.
The Wakeville Stories
36 Exposures
Scrabble and Tabouli
Hamlet's Lear
Keep Breathing (1-act)
Porch by Moonlight (1-act)
Ophelia Cordelia (1-act)
Limerickle (TYA play, co-author)
The Russian Hut
Baklava (a play for voices)

The Strindberg Project/ Co-Translator with Malin Tybahl
Mr. Bengt's Wife
Playing with Fire

Editor:
Riverine: an anthology of Hudson Valley Writers
WaterWrites: a Hudson River Anthology (co-editor)
A Slant of Light: Contemporary Women Writers of the Hudson Valley (with Jan Zlotnik Schmidt)
Reflecting Pool: Poets and the Creative Process

Paradise Loft
poems by
Laurence Carr

Paradise Loft

Poems by
Laurence Carr

CAPS PRESS
LIGHTWOOD PRESS

Paradise Loft

copyright © 2021 by Laurence Carr
All rights reserved
www.carrwriter.com
larrycarr521@gmail.com

This book, or parts thereof may not be reproduced in any form without permission from the author; exceptions are made for brief excerpts used in published reviews.
For information, please write to:
Lightwood Press
lightwoodpress.com

Cover art by Leticia Ortega Cortes
Spanish translation of *in time* by Leticia Ortega Cortes
Design by Elizabeth Cline

FIRST EDITION
ISBN-13: 978-1-7354410-2-3

ACKNOWLEDGMENTS

Two of the short pieces in "Spirits": "Seamus" and "Olga" appeared as part of the "RO.05 Reading Objects" art exhibition at the Samuel Dorsky Museum of Art, SUNY New Paltz, NY. The texts were based on "The Drunk," a lithograph on paper (1923-24) by George Bellows (1882-1925) and were placed next to the artwork then later published in the catalogue. The three "Spirits" pieces were later published in "Brockhurst Review."

Two of the haiku in "haiku p.m." appeared in "Three Line Poetry, Issue #4."

Some "in time" poems are published in the artbook, *Traverse*, with drawings by Power Boothe. Some pieces have been published in Lightwood magazine (Lightwoodpress.com). Many of the poems have been performed at readings at CAPS (Calling All Poets); Next Year's Words; and Greenkill Gallery, Words Carry Us, and other venues.

My thanks to early readers for their guidance: Gregory Abels, Gary Carr, Thomas Festa, Suzanne Sigafoos, Jan Zlotnik Schmidt, Kay Stuntz, Sarah Wyman.

This book is dedicated to my former students, who continue to inspire me.

An earlier book, *The Wytheport Tales*, explores a fantastical land outside of time through surreal images and dreamscapes. *Pancake Hollow Primer*, a novel in prose and poems, explores the idea of how an old farmhouse and its land can change and recreate a person. A third book, *Threnodies: poems in remembrance*, a portrait gallery of people, known and unknown, interweaves the human comedy. These three volumes were published by Codhill Press, New Paltz, New York, with my thanks and gratitude to publisher David Appelbaum for his continuous guidance on these and other projects.

Paradise Loft is a collection that explores time. Countless writers have shown how time affects the characters within their narratives: Proust, perhaps at the centerpiece, with *In Search of Lost Time*, Virginia Woolf with *The Waves* and *Orlando*, and the overlooked but intriguing Lord Dunsany fantasy-romance, *The King of Elfland's Daughter*. In *Paradise Loft*, poems are arranged into nine sections beginning with a prologue: "God's Diary/Day 5", a timeless timeframe. It is followed by "Wording/Morning", thoughts on morning writing; "Journeyman I", a sequence of time-travels; "Feline Dreams" on the afterlives of cats, ending with the mid-20th century romance, "The Ballad of Henrietta Pussycat and Her Lover Thief Coyote." Next, "Even She" are studies, much like an artist might keep in a sketchbook. The prose poems in "time past" bring up collected memories that have lingered long enough to record. "Journeyman II" continues the time-travels, and "Wording/Evening" shows the end of day grasping at end of day thoughts. The book closes with "in time": seven dreamscapes conjure themselves between two and seven A.M. and bring on a new beginning.

TABLE OF CONTENTS

Prologue	1
God's Diary/Day 5	2
Wording/Morning	5
sharpened pencils	6
haiku a.m.	7
scraps	8
in the salvation army parking lot	9
pencils write a line of words	10
On the Poet's Walk	11
Journeyman I	13
above the mast	14
striding through sand	15
Prometheus & Sisyphus	16
no matter	17
the comet approaches	18
Feline Dreams	21
her 10th life	22
in her mirror she sees herself	24
her haunt	25
The Ballad of Henrietta Pussycat And Her Lover-Thief Coyote	27
Even She	31
her up of down	32
like a nude descending a staircase (in 3)	33
Red Cup	36
breath	38
the mystery of melancholy	39
Lakeside	40

Time Past — 41
    Baggage (the things he carried) — 42
    Queen City Show: New Yorkers on film, (Poughkeepsie, 1912-1917) — 43
    Spring Thaw — 45
    Harlequin — 47

Spirits - Seamus, Olga and Stephano — 49
    Seamus — 50
    Olga — 52
    Stephano — 53

Journeyman II — 55
    in the field — 56
    tea ceremony #12 — 57
    and what will become of the nighttime sky — 58
    the comet arrives — 59
    a short history of the universe — 60

Wording/Evening — 61
    the card game — 62
    haiku p.m. — 63
    writing at the moment of the winter solstice — 64
    Your Shelf — 65

in time
    2 a.m. — 68
    3 a.m. — 69
    4 a.m. — 70
    5 a.m. — 71
    6 a.m. — 72
    7 a.m. — 73

Bios
    Laurence Carr   74
    Leticia Ortega   75

Calling All Poets   76

PROLOGUE

God's Diary/Day 5

and before that which was
there was
this passing think
of somethink

we pass into
thoughts outside
then turn around and
thereitisagain

that bracky little mustard seed
there in our sandalshoe
that rubs us into a makepeace
make me image
now & here
to stand before me ever after

a spit of clod
that will never dissolve away
the That that never was before
but now becomes our once and willbe
that somethink that
we into he into she into
they themselves can upright stand
and never falter kneeward →

then pass them into Paradisical
eye to I a gain

and let their eye teeth and strawfoots
touch their selves
two ends a gain the middle

and with cedar shaky feetfalls
we'll draw them forth with starry stuff
to seep no longer never
from their lowly low loin darkness
to be a now at one with us
and wander forth to
sing our eden song

Wording/Morning

sharpened pencils

their shavings left behind

these particles of trees who
make their way to compost piles

and with the heat and wet turn back to earth
where everything worth anything returns

paper pencil
hand and thought

a foursome plays
in soft rebellion

haiku a.m.

pencil etches pulp
the match strikes, the tinder sparks
distant fires glow

    fingers brush the keys
    currents sail the bark downstream
    t'ward an unknown shore

scraps

on the backs of grocery lists
scribble early drafts of poems

on the backs of early drafts
record the groceries for the week

a palimpsest of sustenance

in the salvation army parking lot

i meet a fellow poet
for a swap of
slant rhyme chat

the perfect place
to find salvation

      inside—
we find a dogearred brittle book
of verse and
snappy epigrams on teeshirts XXL

      outside—
there's graffiti
on the western wall—
a scatological ode

with a little craft, it could read
in heroic couplets but in this draft

it advertises genitalia
with all its useful uses

pencils write a line of words

and in their time and space wear down

and just like us
turn dull from overwork

but unlike us
dive headfirst into sharpeners

grind back to life,
their point of view renewed

then dance on teeter-totter tables
in a coffee house of caffeine rings
with writing paper, bridal white,

a waltz of words reveals lost truths,
confessions left unspoken.

On the Poet's Walk

You may have heard all this before.
Or maybe in a dream.

A poem leads you down a path where light
can filter through. To a place where
truth and time sit silently together.

You can hear them speaking faintly,
but they never catch your eye.

They'll toss a word or phrase your way
that somewhere you've misplaced.

And when all is said,
they'll send you on your way.
Back to the place you live your life.

And once you're there, you'll see
all sorts of things you've missed.
The mirror gazing back.
The darkness without dread.
The face of the one from long ago.

They now belong to you.
These words, these gifts
to keep or give away.

Journeyman I

above the mast

above the spire

the sleepless wanderer floats
thru curls of umbraed waves

the path to outland dreams
ascends thru night's soft skin

to enter open pores of sleep
where comfort still abounds

and the mind's eye reveals
and shakes a hundred truths
from doubt

striding through sand

firm footfalls press
on beach glass sand

two sun-baked hands
dance ancient rhymes
that jar a seabird's path

words waft on breaths
with where, and when
and glyph the stones with why

Prometheus & Sisyphus

the old god and king could have cut their losses and
saved infinite time had they used the same rock

one chained to its face adding some muscle
while the other heaved it up that incline

together they could've carried out
their master plan to end eternity

and like all who pass through here
to live their hallowed lives
in sacred myths

some end up etched in stone
some singed in stars
while some of us are gifted other things

no matter

the number of branches and boughs
stacked on the stickpile fence
                it neither rises nor sinks—

a palisade of broken trees
cut short by hail and wind
                the weight of snow
                the clutch of disease
                and boring bugs

the eastwest fence has retained
        its height, its length and breadth
            throughout the years—
a certainty through times uncertain
this permanence of latitude in an age
            outside our own

the comet approaches

we see your tail exhaling fire
      an inverted dragon
      with eyes stone cold
      in a face of anguish

barely holding that distant
memory of your jailbreak
seven sister states away

      you're on the lam
      skidding through the
      outer banks of nothing

the nomad's
timeless cries pierce
the pinprick holes of heaven

      the immigrant
      igniting a mobius path
      that holds dark secrets →

the refugee
outrunning the firestorm
that consumes your every moment

> as you come near
> we're haunted by
> your presence

our walls build up
suspicions grow
marvel turns to dread

you're in our crosshairs
 (just in case)

Feline Dreams

her 10th life

her shadow floats
across the rug diffused
through west bay sunsets

and for a moment
she's a presence until
the moment when she isn't

I see her—but it's only a pile
of sock strewn laundry
on the closet floor

I hear her in the midnight
creak of floorboards that
catch her tone and timbre

phantoms live among us
more comfortable with you
than you with them

she has no thought of leaving
no reason really
and little inclination →

this house has always been
more hers than mine
she owns the deed

and time which
ticks me off is no longer
part of her routine

she no longer lifts soft paws
but glides from room to room
her footsteps even lighter now

a shade of former self
an imprint a remembrance
of all she ever was and all
she is and all she leaves behind

in her mirror she sees herself

The collarless cat and the catless collar still waft
through these woods outside of time and space.

Once wide-eyed wild, then tamed but
always yearning to accordion herself
out of her necklace of submission.

Once fashioned to priss on dainty pillows.
Until—in her defining moment,
she walks past the floor length
mirror to reclaim her genes long buried.

Arching now in tomcat pose, she shreds her pettycoat
party dress—forced to don for holiday family photos.
Paws soon open the outside door to shatter civil laws.
Her shackle-necklace springs open
on a white pine's hanging bough.
Free now, never to return.

Epilogue:
That fragment of collar will be discovered by future tenants
when they walk the property. A shard of dim and distant past,
its meaning now lost. But the several elders who remain will
hold the fading memory of that lioness incarnate who will roam
these woods forever.

the haunt

She's sprouted wings by now
ready for her solo flight
that will finally give her
that bird's eye view she's longed for.

She'll haunt the hill long after we're long gone.
And then move on. The explorer of the unexplored.

Her wings will take her well beyond
our old and narrow world,
closing distance
condensing time
till neither one exists

The Ballad of Henrietta Pussycat and Her Lover-Thief Coyote

1. Seduction

and that was then
        and this is now
and all was odd
        and even
even as the Sands
        pour thru the glass
always half full
        of sweet melody

we'll rally a cry for the
        down and outers
outside in and inside outers
        in our pushme pullyou
carnival bed
        we'll live in Fortune's Eye
in the sweet bye and bye
        where the buys are good
and the goods are plenty

and we'll follow
        each other's nightstalk dreams
and flash in the pan
        to the big band sounds
of Henry Lightfoot
        the swingking of oriental syncopate
over umbrella drinks
        in a bath of Andalusian lime

2. Minds and Bodies

she is the Lasagna Queen
        at the sacred bleeding heart of jesus
street fair— her face painted
        on helium balloons—
she rings out three shots for a quarter
        and the whole world is her kissing booth

he is her cause celeb
        the cause for every rebel
her dreamdate of motorcycle mayhem
        in skintite leather
bellies up to the bar
        two fingers from the top shelf
with his deadeye
        aces and eights smile
to her "don't be stingy baby"
        and she couldn't and wouldn't
for all she knows and all she wants is his

3. Tar Beach

and up they go, up the stairs
        to starlight heaven, up the
fire escape, rusted like heartache
        and pitted like acne
and there on the midnight roof
        with her bang shang a lang
Maybelline eyes
        lost in the fog of love
they frictionize themselves
        in a last chance
Going Out of Business
Everything Must Go
Fire Sale

dancing sacred and profane
        arm in arm and eye to eye
        and cheek to cheek
        and back to back
        and belly to belly
till the two into one halve themselves
        and hardwire into nightfire porcelain

and their then was then
        and their this is now
and that is all there is
        in the land of love
forever

Even She

her up of down

it's a slippery slope
from cloud high reverence
that zygote of being
of perfect tear
to the skydive
plop and splat
of raw-edged
rorschach blotch

beating on heads and walks
on tongues of slimy toads
and stillborn seeds

but in the heat of night
she reinvents
      a ghostly song
        of see-through mist
she vaporizes away from wouldbe lovers
who watch the sodden lark ascend

like a nude descending a staircase (in 3)

1.

passing bike girl

her   that
in   her who
her stratospheric
      yes
a make her
path across
      herself
in selfless
      what is
maker made

the her
      the even she
of she and me

2.

queen of the night

she wears liz's purple eyes
    her purple mane
    her redblue state

her purple lips
    a lapping pool
electric charge
    of grape froze fruit
a slurp of royal passion

3.

first bloom

of yes
and no
the eyes
of yes
the ides
of no
and then

perhaps

a shudder
into
no thing else
a maybe
baby
may be
not
or may be
some
thing
still

Red Cup

That red cup broke yesterday.
>a touchstone given to me
>ages ago

and with no warning
>it's sifting through your fingers
>like sand on a cape cod beach

>goddam gravity
>taking everything
>like it has
>all the time in the world
>coming out of nowhere

There ought to be a law.
>it's grand theft really

That cup
crafted by some maker
whose name I've forgotten.
>a one of a kind piece
>a little off center a little odd
>but that's what made it the cup of
>choice and not some random vessel. →

It filled its cosmic place.
I thought it would certainly outlast me.
    me the transient
     the cup immortal
But we're all starstuff, I suppose
in that race that races to the end.

    and who would believe
    that cup
    edging the shelf above the sink
    would cross the finish line
    before the rest of us

breath

breathe out the past that coats the throat
breathe in the what remains
breathe out the you denied and lost
breathe in our song's refrain

breathe in the mist
of unseen sight
breathe out the crackled shell
breathe in my friend
my love
my self

breathe in
the breath
of us

the mystery of melancholy

like de Chirico's daughter
she hooprolls down
blind alleyways

awaiting a body
who will hold her
closer than a lover.

Lakeside

I can take that morning chill
that drifts up off the lake.

The next breeze will bring
another degree of warmth

and with each exhale
a micro-surge of bodyheat.

The mist burns off.
The veil that holds all doubts

in those early unclocked moments
lifts. Earth and water reveal themselves.

Then you behind the moisture
on the glass looking out at me.

TIME PAST

Baggage (the things he carried)

His duffle stores necessities:
extra underwear, the folding toothbrush,
warmer socks. It holds a book he'll never read,
but might scan when there's nothing else, like that
random person at a party who's suddenly beside you.

The bag sometimes holds a second book he read
so long ago he forgot the gist, but remembers
somewhere that it changed him and wonders
if it would again.

It holds a folded scrap of paper with the address of someone
he once knew, who he'll probably never see, but could
if he made the effort. But they've probably grown too far
apart except to have that "skim the surface" catchup call.

The bag holds words on pages, scraps of thoughts,
vying for attention and knowing that if they could just
clearly state their case, they could unlock the mysteries
that keep him up at night or could conjure up those
things he once believed or doubted.

He's come to believe his body holds his baggage, too.
His socks and shoes, pants, a shirt and underwear.
And a full array of ingested meds to protect him
from himself. From those kind and deadly thoughts,
the ones that heal and slay.

Queen City Show
New Yorkers on film: Poughkeepsie, 1912-1917

Reel 1.

The toothy guy grins at the camera—and the camera loves him back. The Hudson River's leading man—the heartthrob of the hobble skirt cuties who show him some ankle ascending the trolley steps. The beefy stevedore heaves coal to feed the riverboat flexing his mighty pecs and in return collects an array of batting dark eyes and pouty rosebud lips. And all those sporty hats, a haberdasher's dream, set at jaunty angles, atop slicked-back smiles, chasing a tease in feathers, beads and veils.

Reel 2.

Mr. Ryder sells automobiles, the closest thing to foreign travel that some will ever see.
Except for the ones, his sons and their pals who flirt their way down Market or Main—
who within weeks, will stride into the Enlistment Office, through a smoke screen of Lucky Strikes where they'll exchange their duds for goggle-eyed masks to quell the mustard gas, a fog of war no one will explain. Then in jig time a short goodbye for that's the long and short of it—Off to The Big Show, Over There →

Reel 3.

Doe-eyed doughboys trade their dashing two-step for parade march that turns into a run for their lives into No Man's Land. Beyond the wire toward their German brothers, their cousins and nephews they left behind in the old country but who share their names and genes. Stumbling forward where the old world meets the new. A collide-a-scope of shattered dreams. And all too soon—in that blink of an eye—the going, going, gone. The date-night Nickelodeons, the nickel beers and blind alley kisses. Now, just a maze of Vaudeville trench and volley. Leaving behind a scrap for dearest Ma or the sweetheart who keeps the candle burning. And in that moment before they know it, it's over, over there and they're sent home—and they haven't even seen Paree—

Reel 4.

They won't grow a day older. Loaded like cargo one at a time on leaky old ships like the ones they sailed over on. But at least no one is seasick this time. They're stacked in flag-draped boxes heading home for their hero's welcome where they'll take jobs as cemetery gardeners, filling holes and seeding earth. And soaking in rain they knew back when. And visited by friends, the left behinds, who pour a beer over their graves for a Saturday night salute. "And no one made better than that old German brewmeister, who was it, old man Hausman… Hauserman… Hausinger. Best beer in the city. And how he'd sneak us a pint out the back door." And those Saturday nights and the lifting of pints are theirs now forever.

Spring Thaw

The old well pump had been frozen since
the fifth of November. She remembers the date.
It was the day he left and said he would be
"out of reach" for a while.

She tried the pump again in January: but nothing.
And now it's April. Is it the first, April Fool's Day
when he used to play some trick?

The water trickled very little for all that pumping.
But tomorrow they'll be a steadier stream. And then
a gush in a week's time. Water enough to fill the old,
patched tub so she could take a proper bath.

And that would be the day the postman would come
around the bend. And the flow of letters would
start up again. Slowly. One by one, like the drip by
drip of the spring thaw.

She'd peer out the front window to see him coming
down the path. Some of those letters would be postmarked
from a place she didn't know. →

And she'd read the first one in her bath. With water as hot
as she could stand. Kettle after kettle heated
on the wood stove. Mixing with the cold well water
from deep down in the earth. Where she knew part
of her had been living.

She'd read the letter slowly. Word by word, drop by drop.
She'd feel its warmth of words rising up like steam.
And at the end it would ask her something. One question.

And it would keep her body heated
even as the water cooled.
She wouldn't need the water's heat.
The temperature that
rose up from the folded paper
while she lay in the water was enough
to wrap her in its warmth.
And she would know right then that spring would
start up life again. That all of this would happen.
And should. And would.

Harlequin

The old carousel was carted away. It now sits in a backlot,
on the other side of a fence in the oldest part of
Playland Park awaiting its next life.

Harlequin's face is carved twenty odd times on the top edge
of the canopy, cracked and flaking away.
When the wheel spun, those twenty green faces looked out
in every direction and they became one.

A calliope stood at the center and ran on a breath of steam.
Exhaling melodies that could be whistled by those who
remembered even if they'd forgotten the words.

Over the years, the jester heard all the wishes
of all of his visitors under his roof. The ones who ride
his noble horses and reach for the ring and the ones
who watch hypnotized by the spin of his wheel.

He held his silent, cold stare with lips that could turn
to a smile, but never did. He stayed as constant
as the day he was carved. He's missed nothing,
he remembers it all. His curse and his joy.

And now waits for the day when someone will come
and restore him back to the timeless path.
That ongoing orbit where we meet ourselves again.

Spirits
Seamus, Olga and Stephano

Seamus

Their son was paid in hooch and drove
the whiskey wagon from the wharf to the warehouse.
He told his father that he would earn enough
to retrieve Granpap's pocket watch and fob from
Shinman's Pawn Shop. But being paid in hooch,
he was always short.

He started to drink his wages.
And sometimes, not come home
at night. Then, one day, after his run,
he drove off the pier.
They said he misjudged a turn.
Or was it that lowdown pain
when he knew he could
never look the old man in the eye and
hand back the watch. And fob.

His father was told outside
Kosinski's Butcher Shop and
walked home slowly holding the news
like a hod of bricks.
Up the stoop and through the door.
Silent until the door creaked shut and
he faced the four who had to be told. →

His son. Dead of drink they'll say.
But a father knows what kills a son.
The boy, who in his dreams,
would have won the race.
Now gone.
With a father grieving
in a way no one else will know.
Like a falling oak, cleaved in a lightning storm.

Olga

She never gave herself over to America.
The old country never left her. Nor she, it.
She misses the plow and her hands stained
with manure and the blood of brown chickens.
And the smells of wet sheep on rainy mornings.

It's only this now. This fifth-floor walkup.
With their four gray walls. And rusty water.
(When did her feet last touch earth?)

Her young sister-in-law arrived last week.
Another bed in the kitchen. Another mouth.
She waits until they all go out,
then buys rye whiskey
from the gang wages. Then hides the bottle
high atop the maple chest.
She drinks alone.
Imbibes America.
And flies over the moon to that village
she's never left.

Stephano

He crashes in. The Bull from the Sea.
Waves of fists beat the walls
in their leaky attic room.
The landlocked stevedore curses the day
he landed.
"The Big Dumb Greek" of the oily hair
and onyx eyes.

In his lost hours,
he hears the sirens' nocturne.
From the old brick house
the girls on brick alley sing to him.
The seductive caress of Lydian mode.
He can't help himself.
He's fallen under their rapture before.
To be immortal.
Before—this life happened.
This life no longer his.

He'll climb aboard them all and
explore their coastlines.
Bodies of water who let him sink down
never reaching bottom.
Different from everything he knows.
A place so far away from
the dust and stink of the rolling mill.
He'll drink deep from the cask they offer him.
Drink to forget himself. And all the rest.

Journeyman II

in the field

i sometimes stand in cornstalked fields
    slashed by goldbrown razor leaves

I warm my hands with garlicky breath
when dark's first light sneaks up from behind
    and brushes my ears with velvet hands
    and whispers things i knew I knew
    but since have long forgot

leaving me with a corn-mulch crown
    crunched on my head
    where crows can perch
    and caw their mocking
    "majesty"

tea ceremony #12

veiled in bags, a shroud of dust
        these unknown leaves
from unknown climes
        sealed in paper boxes
like old tut's poor relations
        their perfume long wafted off
its nose long lost like mr. sphinx

closer now to compost
        than shiny leaves in tropic air
we drink in memory
        of those past days
when we held the chariot's reins

and what will come of the nighttime sky

and what will become of us
when we look into it with longing

into the brilliance of its darkness
        that plenitude unseen

when all the stars extinguish or at least
        draw their cosmic curtains

when everything above matches
        everything below
like those ebony sands we walked upon

the beach at Perissa Lavina
        and Vik Papenoo

on those nights when we
        connected dots and were
each other's constellations

the comet arrives

when our pathways cross
and our guiding lights converge
will we see in you a carbon copy
and invite you in as honored guest
or explode you into heaps of slag
swirled into outer orbits

another stumbling misstep—
a knowing look
a soft caress
a lover's waltz
another chance
we'll never know

a short history of the universe

the stars will stay on all night long
when someone down below
cries out to them

they will stay on all night long
if even one of us fears sleeping
in the dark

the stars will not shut off at night
when even one of us
feels lost

Wording/Evening

the card game

we write our lives on little cards
to file away the past
a memory of what came first
and what comes next

our present
is a flat, blank space
not chronicled yet
by the chronicler's hand

white silent snow
the white of
summer light

until that moment we fill the card
with present past
skimming our pens from edge to edge
until our ink runs dry

haiku p.m.

pencils skate on sheets
wood on wood like skin to skin
the lovers renew

pen chases paper
words inflame the writer's heart
they seek nothing else

writing at the moment of the winter solstice

1 a.m.
I am

Your Shelf

As you trudge toward that place you need to be,
you could take along a favorite book to pass the time.
And in that deeper reading for the second, third,
or umpteenth time, the lives inside their world and
yours begin to interweave. And what was once your
solo voyage is now a grand entwining tour.

These old friends, who know you like a book.
You're sequels now on a winding path
of never-ending story.

in time

2 a.m.

by the time I was born
the gods had departed
the ones
once so present
were gone
leaving only memories
etched in the old stone tablets
nearly erased by the rain

2 a.m.

para cuando nací
los dioses se habían ido
aquellos
siempre presentes
habían partido
dejando sólo memorias
grabadas en la antigua piedra
casi borradas por la lluvia

3 a.m.

in the morning
a morning song
at evening
an evening song
in the waning heat of day
notes sleep inside
the wooden flute and await
their breath

3 a.m.

por la mañana
un canto matutino
por la tarde
un canto vespertino
en el menguante calor del día
las notas duermen dentro
de la flauta y anticipan
su respiro

4 a.m.

time travels
inside the traveler
each step a second
each journey
a life until
time and the traveler
stop together
at rest at the oasis

4 a.m.

el tiempo viaja
dentro del viajero
cada paso un segundo
cada camino
una vida hasta que
tiempo y viajero
paran a la vez
al descanso del oasis

5 a.m.

there's a time
to understand everything
and a time to understand
nothing
and the
journey ends when neither is
present and the gift of time
is given

5 a.m.

hay un tiempo
para entenderlo todo
y hay un tiempo para entender
nada
y el
viaje termina cuando ninguno
está presente y el regalo del tiempo
ha sido dado

6 a.m.

in time
we learn the which
and why
we learn the what
we think and do
but only afterwards
do we learn
the learning

6 a.m.

con tiempo
aprendemos el cual
y porqué
aprendemos el que
pensamos y hacemos
pero sólo después
aprendemos
lo aprendido

7 a.m.

we set time back
and then ahead
time runs fast
or slow and then runs out
we travel time through life
and whether we know it or not
we have all the time in the world

7 a.m.

atrasamos el tiempo
y después lo adelantamos
el tiempo vuela
o se frena y después se acaba
viajamos el tiempo en vida
y lo notemos o no
tenemos todo el tiempo del mundo

LAURENCE CARR lives in New York's Hudson Valley and writes fiction, CNF, poetry and plays. His novel, *Pancake Hollow Primer*, (Winner: Next Generation Indie Book Award for first novel) and two poetry collections, *Threnodies: poems in remembrance* and *The Wytheport Tales* are published by Codhill Press. As anthology editor at Codhill, he edited or co-edited four anthologies: *Riverine: An Anthology of Hudson Valley Writers; WaterWrites: A Hudson River Anthology; A Slant of Light: Contemporary Women Writers of the Hudson Valley* (Winner of the USA Best Book Award for Fiction Anthology); and *Reflecting Pool: Poets and the Creative Process* (Finalist in Non-Fiction, Next Generation Indie Book Awards). Over 20 of his plays for adult and young audiences have been produced in New York City, regionally and in Europe including the Off-Broadway *Kennedy at Colonus* (cited in the *Burns Mantle Best Plays Series*) and his play for voices, *Baklava*, now archived at WNYC radio after playing on "Airworks" for National Public Radio and in Bratislava on Slovak Public Radio. In Europe, *36 Exposures* premiered in Prague and *Food for Bears* premiered in Warsaw. His writing has appeared in numerous publications. Laurence taught creative and dramatic writing at SUNY New Paltz for over twenty years where he was named a Teacher of the Year. In 2020, he created the online magazine Lightwood at Lightwoodpress.com. Please visit at: www.carrwriter.com

LETICIA ORTEGA CORTES is a visual artist born in Mexico and based in New York City. She divides her practice between the city and the Hudson Valley where she embraces her love for nature.

Ortega has mastered different media including oil painting, watercolor, sculpture, printmaking, and installation. She has exhibited solo a number of times in the United States and Mexico including John Davis Gallery in NY and Museo de las Culturas in Coahuila. Her work was selected in the Biennial Olga Costa I. She is recipient of numerous prestigious awards including Vitro Art Center in Monterrey and the Coahuila State Arts Grant in Mexico. Her work is found in public and private collections.

Ortega is also an art educator, founder and director of Wet Paint! Art Studio in NYC. She is co-founder and curator of several cultural centers and galleries including Galería NIX in Saltillo, and NIX NY art space, the window, and Front art space in NYC.

She holds art studies from Parsons School of Design, Cooper Union and School of Visual Arts in NYC, and a Bachelor's degree in Architecture from Coahuila State University in Mexico.

CALLING ALL POETS (CO-PUBLISHER)

I have, over the course of CAPS' twenty-two years, employed much hyperbole and eloquent shadings both in the press and in person to discuss our ideals, our perseverance, our ultimate goal. I've hyper-used such words and vague concepts like democratic forum, free speech, community, camaraderie, open mic, diversity, etc.

But when you pare it down, as any poet should, (as Larry certainly does in *Paradise Loft*) it comes down to one North Star constant.

Tell it. Mean it.
Make us wonder. Make us think.
Make us believe.
Welcome to the fold.

Mike Jurkovic - Prez, Calling All Poets Series.

www.ingramcontent.com/pod-product-compliance
Lightning Source LLC
Chambersburg PA
CBHW060408080526
44583CB00012B/505